Wanda -

You are a very special young man to our family. May God bless you and Lynn in all that you do and in all of life —

Love —

Peg W.

June 8, 2007

TAKING CARE OF THE BASICS

101 SUCCESS FACTORS FOR MANAGERS

BY
DAVIS WOODRUFF, PE, CMC

Management Methods, Inc.
P.O. Box 1484 Decatur, AL 35602
Tel: 256-355-3896 Fax: 256-353-3140
davisw@managementmethods.com
www.managementmethods.com

1663 LIBERTY DRIVE, SUITE 200
BLOOMINGTON, INDIANA 47403
(800) 839-8640
WWW.AUTHORHOUSE.COM

This book is a work of non-fiction. Unless otherwise noted, the author and the publisher make no explicit guarantees as to the accuracy of the information contained in this book and in some cases, names of people and places have been altered to protect their privacy.

© 2005 Davis Woodruff. All Rights Reserved.

No part of this book may be reproduced, stored in a retrieval system, or transmitted by any means without the written permission of the author.

First published by AuthorHouse 08/04/2005

ISBN: 1-4208-7618-X (e)
ISBN: 1-4208-4620-5 (sc)t

Library of Congress Control Number: 2005907103

Printed in the United States of America
Bloomington, Indiana

This book is printed on acid-free paper.

PREFACE

If you're tired of philosophy and buzzwords, or if you don't really like to read management books this one is for you! Since 1984 clients have been telling me, "we like your common sense, back to the basics, focus on the fundamentals approach." So, the time has come to share these timeless and basic success factors with you.

For a no-nonsense approach to managing and leading your organization, study and apply these 101 success factors. Use the tools in the appendix to help you focus on and apply what you've learned.

As for the verses to consider, my prayer is that each one who reads this book will take the time to look up the references and attempt to understand and apply the principles to your work as a manager.

Have fun becoming a more effective manager!

Davis M. Woodruff, PE, CMC
President
Management Methods, Inc.
Decatur, AL
Summer 2005

> "the gift of God is eternal life."
> -Romans 6:23

DEDICATION

This work is dedicated to all who have helped me grow as a leader and manager. The one who has helped me grow the most is my wife, Lynn, without whom this work would never have been possible. She has supported my efforts in all of our business endeavors, in times of uncertainty and difficulties as well as in the good times. My ultimate thanks is to my Heavenly Father who gave me the ability to prepare this work. This book is dedicated to His Glory.

Davis Woodruff
Decatur, AL
Summer 2005

Table of Contents

Achievement 1
Action 2
Alternatives 3
Attitude 4
Balance 5
Barriers 6
Behavior 7
Belief 8
Budgets 9
Change 10
Commitment 11
Communication 12
Customer 13
Data 14
Decisiveness 15
Delegation 16
Details 17
Discipline 18
Employees 19
Empowerment 20
Evaluation 21
Expectations 22
Facts 23
Failures 24
Fairness 25
Follow-Up 26
Future 27
Generosity 28
Go 29
Goals 30
Habits 31
Harassment 32
Honesty 33
Humility 34
Information 35

INITIATIVE	36
INNOVATION	37
INTEGRITY	38
JARGON	39
JEALOUSY	40
JOBS	41
JUSTICE	42
KEEP	43
KINDNESS	44
LEADERSHIP	45
LEARN	46
LEAVE	47
LISTEN	48
MANAGEMENT	49
MEASUREMENT	50
MONEY	51
MOTIVATION	52
NEGLECT	53
NEVER'S	54
NEW	55
NOTICE	56
OBSERVE	57
ONCE	58
ORGANIZING	59
OVERKILL	60
PERFORMANCE	61
PLANNING	62
PREPARATION	63
PROCEDURES	64
PROCESSES	65
QUALITY	66
QUANDARIES	67
QUESTIONS	68
REGULATIONS	69
REINFORCEMENT	70
RELATIONSHIPS	71
RESOURCES	72

Respect	73
Resolve	74
Results	75
Serve	76
Sincerity	77
Solutions	78
Staffing	79
Teach	80
Technology	81
Termination	82
Time	84
Understanding	85
Uncertainty	86
Values	87
Variation	88
Vision	89
Waste	90
Willingness	91
Wisdom	92
Work	93
eXceptions	94
eXpectations	96
eXpenses	97
Yes	98
Yesterday	99
Yielding	100
Youth	101
Zeal	102
Zip	103
Summary	104
Endnotes	105
My Success Plan	106

Achievement   *Success Factor 1*

Working Definition: Getting things done and meeting goals. Accomplishment.

Success Factor: Successful managers focus their organization on achievement as opposed to activities.

Application: Be sure that your employees know what's expected and measure their accomplishments against the goals that have been established. Reinforce them for meeting goals.

Verses to Consider: Ecclesiastes 6:3, Psalm 37:4-5

Being More Successful: Do my employees know when they have accomplished the goals we've established? How well do I communicate achievements within the work group? Take the time to celebrate significant achievements by your employees.

To Do: What can you do to achieve more each day, especially in the area of management and leadership? Do it.

Notes:

Davis Woodruff, PE, CMC

ACTION   *Success Factor 2*

Working Definition: Moving from plans to execution of plans; or, getting things done!

Success Factor: Planning is important and required of successful leaders, however, just as important is the action to get it done. Diligently executing our plans with enthusiasm and attention to detail can make the difference between success and failure. Sometimes it seems safer not to act, but remember a ship is safe in the harbor, but it was built to sail the seas. Taking actions based on solid plans or other information is what we're paid to do as managers.

Application: The difference in success and failure is timely action. For example, procrastination is an action that will lead to failure!

Verses to Consider: Proverbs 12:11, Ecclesiastes 11:4,6

Being More Successful: What plans or objectives do you have for your work group? Are you taking action steps to achieve the desired results?

To Do: List several positive actions you can take this week towards achieving your goals and objectives.

Notes:

ALTERNATIVES   *Success Factor 3*

Working Definition: Different potential courses of action to reach a solution to a problem, work place situation or to achieve an objective.

Success Factor: Focus is important, but managers need to practice developing alternatives when faced with problems or situations in the work place. Developing reasonable alternatives enables us to identify multiple approaches to a specific issue or situation. Practicing the discipline of developing alternatives will make you a better problem solver for your organization.

Application: In most situations faced by a manager, there are multiple possible solutions or actions. The effective manager will develop alternatives that will enable him to approach problems more objectively as opposed to being "fixed" on one solution or course of action. Encouraging those who report to you to bring several alternatives when discussing problem situations will build a more competent work force for your organization. This practice will help you develop your people.

Verses to Consider: Proverbs 21:30; Proverbs 29:30

Being More Successful: Are there product problems, process issues, service issues or people issues facing your organization? List the top three or four.

To Do: Identify at least three alternatives to each of the problems or issues listed above.

Notes:

Davis Woodruff, PE, CMC

ATTITUDE *Success Factor 4*

Working Definition: How we view and respond to people, situations and events.

Success Factor: We choose how we respond to the people, situations and events that occur at work (as well as life in general). The choice is yours—positive or negative; optimistic or pessimistic. The people who report to you will "catch your attitude." Be aware of how you respond, because your people will respond the same way or worse. If you get angry or are usually negative when unexpected situations occur, your employees will soon see that you are not made aware of such situations!

Application: Remember, it's not what happens, but rather how you choose to respond that makes a difference.

Verses to Consider: Philippians 4:11; Colossians 3:23

Being More Successful: Think of recent unpleasant situations in your workplace. How have you responded? Are you generally positive or negative? Are employees willing to approach you with problems?

To Do: Take two steps this week to improve your attitude and the attitudes of those who report to you. List them here and get it done.

Notes:

Balance *Success Factor 5*

Working Definition: Juggling the different roles and priorities in your life and work.

Success Factor: In today's society we have managed to get our priorities somewhat out of order. Let's get back to the basics with our priorities and we will be more successful managers. The priorities in life should be more related to relationships than things or positions. For example, priorities should be our faith, family and work in that order. When these are properly balanced we can be more effective in our role as a leader or manager. Now, in the workplace our priorities need to focus on people, safety, regulatory compliance, quality and housekeeping. When these are in proper balance production will take care of itself.

Application: When priorities are out of balance, then our juggling act will not be successful.

Verse to Consider: Matthew 6:33

Being More Successful: List your priorities in life and then list your specific priorities in the work place. Place them in order of importance to you.

To Do: Using the list above, identify specific ways you can balance your priorities.

Notes:

Davis Woodruff, PE, CMC

Barriers   *Success Factor 6*

Working Definition: Something that "gets in the way" of getting the work done on time and satisfactorily.

Success Factor: Barriers may come in the form of restrictive procedures, mis-interpreted customer or regulatory requirements, organizational roles, job descriptions and "baggage" in relationships.

Application: Learn the barriers to your effectiveness and to the effectiveness of your people and take the appropriate steps to eliminate the barriers.

Verses to Consider: Jeremiah 32:17; Hebrews 12:1-2

Being More Successful: Identify the top barriers in your organization or work group related to production, maintenance, purchasing, quality, procedures, timeliness or relationships.

To Do: Eliminate the barriers you identified.

Notes:

Behavior   *Success Factor 7*

Working Definition: The way one "acts" in the workplace. A textbook definition is "an activity that can be seen, measured or described." [1]

Success Factor: As a manager, your behavior is observed by many people. Thoughtless actions can destroy a career. For example, a manager who loses his temper and throws a hardhat through a processing area will lose the respect of his employees.

Application: Watch your behavior. As a wise first grade teacher once said, "remember who you are and where you are."[2]

Verses to Consider: Proverbs 12:2; Luke 6:31

Being More Successful: Have you been aware of those behaviors that may negatively affect the people who report to you, for example temper, tasteless jokes, casual comments, threats?

To Do: List changes you can make your behavior that will have a positive impact in your workplace.

Notes:

BELIEF

Success Factor 8

Working Definition: Conviction and confidence about "intangibles" in the workplace.

Success Factor: All employees need to have the belief that "the job I do really matters" and that together we can meet the challenges of today, tomorrow, next week and next year. Managers must demonstrate their belief in the people in the organization by training them properly and delegating meaningful work to each person.

Application: Management is responsible for nurturing employee beliefs about the importance of each person and each job.

Verses to Consider: James 1:4-8

Being More Successful: What are your basic beliefs about the company, the people who work for you, and the role you fill each day as a manager?

To Do: Communicate your beliefs to your people. Act accordingly.

Notes:

BUDGETS *Success Factor 9*

Working Definition: Spending plans that help us utilize our resources properly.

Success Factor: Budgets are often considered "dream sheets" or in the worst case one gets an edict of "$X for your department or facility" without really looking at resource requirements related to people, facilities or infrastructure.

Application: When preparing budgets look at resource requirements and establish a realistic spending plan for your organization. What is realistic? Generally, affordable is the criteria! Allocate your financial resources according to the priorities of the organization. Budgets need to take into account internal as well as external factors. External factors may be related to customers, suppliers, changing regulatory requirements or the general economy. Internal factors are generally related to people (including benefits), processes, equipment, materials, utilities and infrastructure needs. Don't forget to factor in contingencies.

Verse to Consider: Proverbs 11: 4; Proverbs 21:5

Being More Successful: Develop a list of the categories you will use to determine your resource allocations and spending plans for the coming year.

To Do: Determine the priorities for your spending plan and the % of the total that could go to each area of your budget. Live within the budget or justify changes in the coming year.

Notes:

CHANGE — Success Factor 10

Working Definition: Doing things differently. One of the constants in business today.

Success Factor: A friend has told me of a sign in his office: "**Change** people, or change **People**." We must realize that change is a constant today. The driving forces of change are cost, competition, technology and regulatory requirements. There are common roadblocks to change that we can all relate to, such as "we've never done it that way before" or "it won't work here." Our job as managers is to manage everyday in such a way as to build trust among our people and then when change is required the foundation is already in place. Change may be internally or externally driven and be operational or strategic. Know for sure that the first rule of change is "somebody ain't gonna like it" and the second rule is "somebody else ain't gonna like it."

Application: Staying ahead of strategic change and managing operational change is one of the critical roles of management today. Be aware that in most organizations change is generally accepted slowly and new ideas are not usually readily accepted.

Verse to Consider: Hebrews 13:8

Being More Successful: What changes have occurred in your organization within the past six months? What changes are planned for the next year?

To Do: Using the changes from the past six months, identify where opposition has taken place and the outcomes of the changes. Next, focus on the changes planned for the coming year and list the steps you can take to insure successful change.

Notes:

Commitment — *Success Factor 11*

Working Definition: "Staying the course" even in the face of adversity.

Success Factor: Too many managers fail to "stay the course." They become "wishy-washy", "see which way the wind is blowing", or chase the "latest and greatest fad." Carefully define your objectives and be committed to attaining them (see Resolve, success factor #74).

Application: Be committed to doing your part in helping your organization meet or exceed customer expectations and to be continually improving. This also means being committed to helping your employees be more effective on their jobs.

Verses to Consider: Joshua 24:15; Proverbs 24:10; Habakkuk 3:17-18

Being More Successful: Do you know what's expected and what the goals are for your department or company? How do you demonstrate your commitment each day to both your employees and your organization?

To Do: Implement actions that will demonstrate your commitment to your company goals and to your employees.

Notes:

COMMUNICATION — *Success Factor 12*

Working Definition: Exchanging information and understanding among people. In some organizations the most significant problem is the lack of exchanging information and understanding in a timely manner.

Success Factor: People in an organization need to "know what they need to know when they need to know it." Most managers think they are great communicators when in reality we are not. We are usually good at providing information in great quantities without checking for understanding or without regard for timeliness. Yet, people often fail to get the information they need when they need it.

Application: The effective manager will focus on improving their communications skills and be sure to check for understanding when passing along information throughout the organization. It's been my experience that in most organizations communications/information flow is generally not as good as management thinks it is.

Verses to Consider: Proverbs 12:18; Proverbs 15:1; Matthew 5:37

Being More Successful: Think of recent communications foul-ups in your organization. Be honest, we've all had them. What could have been done differently to prevent the problem? Spend more time face to face with your people working to improve relationships and communications than in communicating with them via e-mail. Also, be careful of what you say to whom!

To Do: List several immediate action steps you can take to improve communications processes in your organization and to improve your personal communications skills.

Notes:

Customer — Success Factor 13

Working Definition: Anyone who receives something from you, whether internal to your business or outside your business.

Success Factor: It's important that you know your customers. As a manager you have many, from employees in your company to people who buy your goods and services.

Application: Learn your customers—who they are, what they need and what they like because without them you aren't needed! Treat them right!

Verses to Consider: Proverbs 20:10; Proverbs 22:29; Colossians 3:17

Being More Successful: Do you know your customers, what they like and what they want? Have customer requirements been defined and documented? List your top 3—5 customers and what they want or require from you.

To Do: Take two positive steps this week to improve customer service. Do it again next week and the next. Make it a habit to practice improving customer service.

Notes:

DATA   *Success Factor 14*

Working Definition: Numbers or facts about people, processes or products that can be converted to useful information.

Success Factor: One of the realities of the work place today is that we have a lot of data but not much information at times. Meaningful data is difficult to obtain in most organizations, but when you get it the answers you are seeking are usually in there somewhere. Oh yes, we have lots of data, but so much of it is really meaningless when it comes to fact-based decision making. In fact, we have so much data that it's sometimes difficult to separate the "pepper from the fly poop." Never forget that most data is only as reliable as the integrity of the person presenting the data, so it's best to question the data and when you think you have it all, ask one more question.

Application: Knowing the five or six key indicators for your business, work group or organization will enable you to know the data that must be gathered to measure results.

Verses to Consider: Proverbs 18:17; Proverbs 27:23

Being More Successful: Identify five or six key indicators that will indicate the "health" of your business or work group. Be sure to list how you could measure each. For example, in a transport company mpg might be one indicator.

To Do: Determine the five or six key indicators you will use to measure results, collect data, analyze results and make action plans for improvement.

Notes:

Taking Care of the Basics

DECISIVENESS *Success Factor 15*

Working Definition: Making effective decisions in a timely manner.

Success Factor: It's a shame when the work force is waiting for managers to stop procrastinating and make decisions. Too often managers delay progress or even worse let a situation force the decision by not making a decision. Workers don't respect indecisive leaders.

Application: Learn and use a systematic process for making decisions. Make effective decisions in a timely manner. For example, define the problem or situation, get the facts, look at the options, get input where appropriate, evaluate the consequences and make a decision.

Verse to Consider: Ecclesiastes 11:4

Being More Successful: What kind of decisions do you make each day? How do they affect the work force or your customers? Do I make decisions in a timely manner? Are people waiting on me to make decisions?

To Do: List several immediate action steps you can take to help you make better decisions in a timely manner.

Notes:

Davis Woodruff, PE, CMC

DELEGATION *Success Factor 16*

Working Definition: Making effective work assignments based on the competencies of your people.

Success Factor: Many managers today are overloaded with work and yet fail to realize the importance of effective delegation. Successful managers know what can and should be delegated, make the assignments and leave their people alone to get the job done. Ineffective managers will take care of many tasks themselves, stay busy and fail to fulfill their role as a manager.

Application: Many times managers just give direction without getting input or checking for understanding. When delegating a task it is essential to know that the employee understands what is to be done. It is difficult to delegate a job, because with delegation comes the right to make a mistake and the manager is still responsible for all that happens in his or her work group. Yet, it is impossible to be a very effective manager when one is trying to do all the work themselves.

Verses to Consider: Exodus 18:21-24

Being More Successful: Think of the items or tasks you are doing today, this week or this month that really should be done by someone else in the organization.

To Do: Determine who else could or should be doing these tasks and make the work assignments accordingly. You may need to invest in developing certain skills in your workers before you can delegate, if so do it.

Notes:

Taking Care of the Basics

DETAILS *Success Factor 17*

Working Definition: The little things that make the difference between success and failure.

Success Factor: The effective manager is careful to take care of the details, especially where employees and/or customers are concerned. Managers must be involved in the details, especially on the big projects. It is a myth that managers can avoid getting involved in the details of the work to be done. The challenge is to avoid getting so deeply involved in details that you bother your people or fail to manage the overall operation or organization.

Application: The big issues in the work place will be resolved, it's the little things that are harder to focus on every day. Remember, when you've got a little rock in your shoe, nothing's right!

Verse to Consider: Proverbs 27:28

Being More Successful: What are the little things you must look after each day? List the five or six that make the most difference to your employees and customers? (i.e. all the paperwork completed on time and correctly; the milk machine working o.k. on night shift, etc)

To Do: Identify what you can do to demonstrate to your employees and customers that you are taking care of the details. Do it.

Notes:

Discipline   *Success Factor 18*

Working Definition: Helping employees be more successful by providing consequences for undesired behavior in the work place.

Success Factor: Most folks work better when they know the boundaries. Safety, Regulatory Compliance, Quality and Productivity are all dependent upon employees behaving according to expectations. There should be well defined consequences for failing to follow the work place policies, procedures or rules. Expectations should be defined and communicated to each employee.

Application: Ignoring behaviors that do not conform to stated policies, procedures or work place rules will lead to lower morale and productivity. Employees expect their managers to provide consequences when necessary. Most employees in a work group already know when someone is not behaving according to stated requirements and expect to see results from their manager.

Verses to Consider: Proverbs 28:13; Romans 6:23

Being More Successful: Have the specific policies, procedures and work rules been defined for your organization? Do employees know what is required or expected? Have consequences been identified for failure to comply?

To Do: List the critical policies, procedure and work rules in your immediate area. Identify and communicate consequences to your employees.

Notes:

EMPLOYEES — *Success Factor 19*

Working Definition: Employees are the most important resource in your business. Employees are those who really get the work done; without whom you would not have a business. They are real people with real hurts, needs and wants as well as competencies that are good for the business.

Success Factor: The effective manager is one who focuses on meeting the needs of employees. Remember that people generally work well together and usually independent of supervision. Sometimes the need is for correction, but most often the need for positive reinforcement. It is impossible to fully separate "home from work." We are not wired that way, so recognize that sometimes external factors can affect how a person does their job on a given day.

Application: Show your respect for every individual in your company. Take time to speak, get to know them and to listen to them. Everyone is important! If you don't believe it, when the janitor is gone and you run out of toilet paper you see who's really important. The CEO can be gone for days and no one really notices, but you notice quickly when the janitor is absent.

Verse to Consider: Matthew 7:12

Being More Successful: Have you been aware of those things you do that may negatively affect the people who report to you, for example temper, tasteless jokes, constant checking on tasks, not delegating? Are you aware of those things you do that may de-motivate your people? What are those simple things you could do to provide positive reinforcement for your employees? Are you aware of external factors that may be having an adverse effect on some of your employees?

To Do: Make a conscious effort to at least speak to each employee everyday. Demonstrate that you value each person.

Notes:

Empowerment — *Success Factor 20*

Working Definition: Providing competent people the freedom to make decisions related to their work and holding them accountable or responsible for the result.

Success Factor: Generally speaking, people like to have "say-so" in their work and the decisions that affect them day to day. The successful manager will allow people to be involved and give them the freedom and responsibility to make the decisions that are within their realm of knowledge and competence,

Application: Know what decisions you must make as the manager and leave the others to your work force.

Verse to Consider: Proverbs 19:11

Being More Successful: Know and communicate to your people the critical decisions that only can be made by you.

To Do: Know the decisions that you will allow your employees to make and then communicate these to each affected person.

Notes:

EVALUATION

Success Factor 21

Working Definition: Reviewing performance factors or results against expected outcomes. What we often fail to do as managers.

Success Factor: When we have identified the key indicators (see #14, data; #30 goals) then we can evaluate performance against those goals using data and information that is relevant to our success. Often we equate evaluation with performance appraisals. The kind of evaluation we're discussing here is the operational kind that will make a difference in our organization's performance.

Application: Evaluating results against stated objectives will lead us along the path of continual improvement using operational data and not opinions or "feelings."

Verse to Consider: Ecclesiastes 12:4

Being More Successful: Now that you have been collecting data about your key indicators, have you evaluated the results? If not, there's no time like now!

To Do: List the corrective actions or continual improvement actions that are needed to make improvements in your results. Now, get it done.

Notes:

# Expectations	*Success Factor 22*

Working Definition: The five or six key requirements that must be met for a person to be successful on their job. This is not a job description of detailed tasks, but rather the major requirements for success on the job.

Success Factor: Every employee has a need and a right to know what their boss expects. Managers have a responsibility to define and communicate expectations for each employee. Failure to do so leads to frustration and poor performance.

Application: An organization doesn't function well with "MRM—mind reading management." People must know what's expected.

Verse to Consider: Micah 6:8

Being More Successful: Do you know what's expected of you? Have you defined expectations for each of your employees? Make a list of each employee and what you expect of them, and communicate your expectations to each one.

To Do: Clearly communicate your expectations to each of your employees.

Notes:

FACTS

Success Factor 23

Working Definition: The "truth" about any situation, process or product.

Success Factor: We have a lot of data today, but sometimes the facts are woefully lacking when it comes time to make decisions. Often we operate based on "myth" or what we've always done instead of on the facts of the situation today.

Application: Get the facts when making decisions or dealing with employee issues. Another thing to remember is that in meetings we often get to the "opinion" stage of discussions rather than getting about the work of gathering the facts. This phase may lead to suppositions that take on an aura of fact and lead us into the wrong decisions or actions. Sometimes we need to adjourn meetings and get to work gathering facts.

Verse to Consider: John 8:32

Being More Successful: Fact based decision making is a critical requirement in today's fast-paced business world. Use technology as a tool to help you gather the facts about processes and products. When dealing with people issues, you may have to lean more on interviews and discussions to obtain facts.

To Do: Operate with facts not opinion or supposition. Figure out where you need more facts and get busy obtaining the necessary data or information.

Notes:

Failures
Success Factor 24

Working Definition: Those events or situations that provide growth opportunities for us when they don't turn out like we expected.

Success Factor: We all fail at times and we choose how we respond to failure. The choice is yours—learn and grow, or become bitter and resentful. The people who report to you will "catch your response to failures." Be aware of how you respond, because your people will respond the same way or worse. If you are bitter your people will become the same way. If you learn and grow, so will your people.

Application: Remember, it's not if we will have failures, but when and how we will respond that marks the difference for the successful manager.

Verses to Consider: Psalm 51:1-19

Being More Successful: Think of recent "failures" in your workplace. How have you responded? Are you willing to learn and grow?

To Do: List two or three failures that you have experienced in recent months or years. What did you learn? How have they helped you grow? Learn and grow or become bitter are your options when facing failures.

Notes:

FAIRNESS   *Success Factor 25*

Working Definition: Being sure that all employees are treated as equals when it comes to policies, procedures, and "special favors."

Success Factor: Whenever employees perceive the manager is "playing favorites" productivity will decline because teamwork is destroyed.

Application: Even though you may like some employees better than others, an effective manager treats all the same when administering policy and making work assignments.

Verses to Consider: Matthew 20:1-16

Being More Successful: Do you treat all employees alike when it comes to the job? Do you have employees that you just like better than others? What do you need to avoid doing or begin doing to eliminate any perceptions of favoritism?

To Do: Identify the steps you need to take to insure fairness for all employees and that will have a positive impact in your workplace.

Notes:

Follow-Up

Success Factor 26

Working Definition: Letting people know you care by seeing that work assignments are properly performed.

Success Factor: Effective follow-up is not "looking over an employee's shoulder," but simply asking or observing how work is progressing. It lets the employee know you care about them and that the work is important. Once I had a manager who would write items in a journal. If he wrote it down, promptly forgot about it and never followed-up. If he just told you to do something but didn't write it in the journal, you could count on follow-up. Of course, we all learned his pattern rather quickly and ignored most of the stuff he wrote in his book.

Application: When the manager doesn't care enough to follow-up, why should the employee care about the work?

Verse to Consider: Ecclesiastes 7:8

Being More Successful: Do you really know the work being done in your department or business? Do you have a list of the work assignments in your area of responsibility? Do your employees know that you care because you follow-up on work assignments with each one? Are you able to follow-up without being "heavy handed?"

To Do: Do you know of items that need your follow-up. If so, go do it.

Notes:

FUTURE

Success Factor 27

Working Definition: Any time after today, or even after this minute of your life.

Success Factor: We cannot manage history we can only manage the present. However, we can prepare for the future so that when it arrives we are ready for the challenges of that day. As a plant manager once told me, "just because you do not have a problem today, it doesn't mean this won't be a problem a month from now."[3] Look ahead and plan for the future. Prepare for the future, don't worry about the future.

Application: Successful managers realize the importance of planning for next week, month quarter and year. Many businesses today develop three year strategic and operational plans with annual reviews and updates. Practice the discipline of looking ahead, anticipating problems and considering the future effects of decisions that are made today.

Verse to Consider: Matthew 6:34

Being More Successful: Do you know what factors in your business need to be reviewed for future effects? What decisions are being made now that can or will affect the future? What potential problems, external or internal, lied ahead for your business? What preventive actions can you take now?

To Do: Identify the 3—5 areas where you need to be planning for next month, quarter or year. Write out your plans with action items and targets. Look for preventive actions you can take now.

Notes:

GENEROSITY — *Success Factor 28*

Working Definition: Being willing to give of yourself and your resources.

Success Factor: When making decisions that affect employees, the effective manager will attempt to approach them from a position of generosity rather than from "what can I get out of this." When employees experience (or perceive) a generous spirit from their leaders, they generally respond with improved morale and productivity.

Application: It has been said, "it is more blessed to give than to receive." Effective managers realize that employees perform better when they don't perceive their management as so cheap they'll "squeeze a nickel 'til the buffalo dies." Employees can see the false economy in many decisions and often question the way top management rewards themselves.

Verses to Consider: Proverbs 11:24; Luke 6:38

Being More Successful: Are your actions demonstrating generosity towards employees? This is especially true in tough times! What simple and inexpensive steps can you take to demonstrate your generosity towards employees?

To Do: Identify three action items that demonstrate generosity in your workplace.

Notes:

Go

Success Factor 29

Working Definition: What managers must do to gather first hand information about people, processes, products, problems or customers.

Success Factor: Too often managers sit in an office working on administrative stuff when they need to be on the shop floor, in a subordinate's office or in a customer's facility gathering first hand knowledge and information about a specific event or issue. It is rather simple: just get up and get out of the office and GO to where whatever is happening whenever possible and practical. In my career there have been cases where plant managers do not even tour their entire facilities during a given month, much less weekly or daily. It's hard to make the time, but managers must go to where the work is being done.

Application: To be successful the manager cannot always depend upon "filtered information" or discount the effect his or her immediate presence will have in a given situation.

Verse to Consider: Nehemiah 2:12

Being More Successful: Where are some places (work related) that you need to GO?

To Do: Make a list of the top three places you need to go this month or this week and calendar the time to GO. Then, GO.

Notes:

Goals
Success Factor 30

Working Definition: Established targets for performance.

Success Factor: Goals and objectives are often not clearly defined or understood. Yet, people work better with clearly defined goals. Organizations function better when goals are structured to enhance teamwork. Be sure that the goals you set are measurable, controllable and do not conflict with other requirements of the work place. Specific goals should flow from your overall business objectives, be deployed throughout the organization and be understood at relevant levels within the organization.

Application: The effective manager helps employees establish specific, measurable and realistic goals that are based on results not activities.

Verse to Consider: Philippians 3:13-14

Being More Successful: What are the goals for your department, work group or business? Are employees involved in goal setting? Do the goals make sense? Does everyone understand the goals? How do the goals relate to your overall business objectives?

To Do: List the steps you can take to establish goals or to improve upon your goal setting process.

Notes:

Habits   *Success Factor 31*

Working Definition: Routine behaviors that occur without us even thinking about them.

Success Factor: Psychologists say it takes 21 days to establish a new habit. Effective managers take an inventory of their habits and determine the new ones they need to develop and the old ones they need to "cull out."

Application: The way we do our work is generally a result of our habits. Be sure you establish work habits that set the proper example for your employees.

Verse to Consider: I Timothy 5:13

Being More Successful: Have you been aware of those work habits that may negatively affect the people who report to you, for example taking too long of a break, being late for work, leaving early, improper speech, failing to return phone calls or respond to e-mail?

To Do: What habits do I need to change, add or eliminate?

Notes:

Davis Woodruff, PE, CMC

Harassment — _Success Factor 32_

Working Definition: Aggravating employees; or "looking over their shoulder." (This is not to be confused with sexual harassment in the work place which is an entirely different and legal issue.)

Success Factor: Managers often unknowingly harass competent employees by constantly asking trivial questions and/or looking over their shoulders closely when a task has been delegated. Supervisors need to delegate and let the folks get the job done in their way. It should go without saying that any form of hostile or sexual harassment must be dealt with immediately by the organization.

Application: Harassment takes many forms, but one prevalent form is in "looking over the shoulder" of competent employees. Let them get the job done.

Verse to Consider: Proverbs 3:21

Being More Successful: Can you think of recent situations where you aggravated or harassed your employees by not letting them get the work done after you'd delegated it to them?

To Do: List the ways in which you might be "harassing" your employees. Make a conscious decision to eliminate these behaviors.

Notes:

HONESTY   *Success Factor 33*

Working Definition: Being real in what you say and do. Simply telling the truth and "walking the talk."

Success Factor: In a survey of several hundred supervisors and managers conducted by our firm[4], honesty was identified as the #1 trait for supervisors and managers. Honesty is an essential requirement for an effective manager. Honesty includes how you deal with information and data as well as personal conversation with employees.

Application: Even in light of events indicating a decline in honesty at the top levels in some companies, we are seeing a return to values based leadership in many organizations today. Honesty is essential in all our dealings with employees, it is not optional.

Verses to Consider: Proverbs 19:9; Proverbs 20:10

Being More Successful: Is there anything I need to do to be more honest with employees, data or information? Do I know of issues related to honesty that need to be addressed?

To Do: Be honest with employees, nothing more and nothing less is acceptable.

Notes:

HUMILITY

Success Factor 34

Working Definition: Knowing that you are not as important as you may want to think you are; you are expendable to your organization.

Success Factor: Positional authority or power may come to you because of your place on an organization chart. However, successful managers realize the most important people in the organization are those who actually get the work done for the customer. Our job as a manager is to help those people get their job done, not to be a self-important spoiled brat. Humility is a character trait that will enable you to do any task required, even if it means picking up paper in the parking lot or emptying the garbage or re-arranging the office furniture. While these may not be the best use of your time, they are not beneath you as a manager. Simply do your job well, do not seek honor or be self-promoting. Let your actions speak for you. By the way, Jesus was the perfect model of humility. Read Philippians 2:1-11 for a better understanding of true humility.

Application: Humility is demonstrated by the way you perform your job and by how you relate to your people each day.

Verses to Consider: Proverbs 16:18; Matthew 23:12; Philippians 2:3-4

Being More Successful: How do you show your humility to your work force? Or, do you think of yourself as more important than you really are?

To Do: Do something today to let your employees see that you don't think of yourself as "Mr. or Ms. Important."

Notes:

INFORMATION   *Success Factor 35*

Working Definition: Knowledge that is gained as a result of having good data or other facts about specific processes, products or situations.

Success Factor: When dealing with people issues, the manager must be sure to have first hand information and not "hearsay." When dealing with process or product issues, it is vital to ask the right questions to insure that you have the correct information. In fact, when you think you know the answer, ask one more question (maybe 2 or 3 depending upon the source of the information). Information needs to be relevant and useful. Sometimes organizations have so much data they actually have very little useful information.

Application: Know what information is essential to your operations each day and have an organized way of gathering, interpreting and communicating that information within the organization.

Verse to Consider: Proverbs 18:17

Being More Successful: What information is essential to you each day?

To Do: List how you will obtain and use the appropriate information about your key processes or products. Gather the information, interpret it and communicate it.

Notes:

INITIATIVE

Success Factor 36

Working Definition: Demonstrating "want to" in the work place.

Success Factor: Effective managers do more than "just get by." They look for ways to do more than is expected or required which is demonstrating "want to." Sometimes we are guilty of squelching the initiative of employees by ignoring their ideas for improvements or changes. We are too quick to give them the reasons their ideas won't work (see Yes, #96).

Application: Laziness and procrastination are two great thieves of success. Initiative is the key to success. "Lazy hands make a man poor, but diligent hands bring wealth."[5]

Verse to Consider: Proverbs 10:4

Being More Successful: How do you demonstrate "want to?" Do you expect your employees to show initiative, then you must also. What do I need to do differently? Have I become lazy or complacent?

To Do: Demonstrate your initiative this week by taking on an extra task that someone else has been doing or that has gone "undone" for several weeks. Encourage your employees to show their initiative by listening and looking for ways to use their ideas or suggestions.

Notes:

INNOVATION <u>*Success Factor 37*</u>

Working Definition: Improving how you get the work done in your business; or improving your products or services.

Success Factor: Doing things the same way year after year is easy, but can be costly. The successful organizations demonstrate innovation by practicing a continual improvement process that works for them. Many today say that continual improvement is slow and innovation is faster, however the reality is they are essentially the same thing. Both are simply finding better, faster, less costly, more useful ways of getting the work done or the product to market. Most innovation that lasts is driven by those who actually do the work. There are exceptions, such as a brand new invention, but in most cases innovation simply involves folks doing the work better each time.

Application: Managers must set the tone in the organization that encourages people to continually look for ways to improve all business processes. That's when you will see the results of innovations in your workplace.

Verses to Consider: Genesis 1:1-3

Being More Successful: What are your four or five key business processes? Have they changed in the past year?

To Do: Identify at least two innovations in each of your key processes. Now, let's get them implemented.

Notes:

INTEGRITY   *Success Factor 38*

Working Definition: Basic character traits that demonstrate our honesty and commitment in all areas of life.

Success Factor: Integrity is a function of "who we are," and is the demonstrated character we show others. Effective managers guard their integrity—it's easy to lose and impossible to recover.

Application: Watch what you say and do. Let integrity guide all your dealings. As a friend once said to me, "don't do anything in your office that you wouldn't want to see in the morning newspaper."[6]

Verses to Consider: Proverbs 10:9; 11:3

Being More Successful: Do I demonstrate integrity to my employees in all that I say and do? Are there questionable behaviors that I need to eliminate?

To Do: Simply act with integrity in all your dealings.

Notes:

JARGON   *Success Factor 39*

Working Definition: Language used in the work place to avoid real communication.

Success Factor: Effective managers communicate clearly. Avoid excessive use of jargon and buzzwords—be straightforward and to the point.

Application: Say what you mean, say it clearly and mean what you say.

Verse to Consider: Matthew 5:37

Being More Successful: Are you prone to lapse into meaningless jargon with employees and others? What can you do to communicate more clearly?

To Do: Make a conscious effort to eliminate needless jargon from your conversation with employees.

Notes:

Davis Woodruff, PE, CMC

JEALOUSY *Success Factor 40*

Working Definition: Petty concerns that someone else is getting what you think is "rightfully" yours.

Success Factor: Worry about yourself and not others. Focus on the things you can control in the workplace and not what others are doing.

Application: Remember, things are not always as they appear on the surface. What looks like a good situation for someone else may not be what it appears. Get rid of jealousy by focusing on the important stuff and not the trivial concerns over who gets what.

Verse to Consider: Proverbs 14:30

Being More Successful: Are there folks of whom you are jealous? What drives the jealousy? Why are you jealous?

To Do: Overcome the jealousies you have at work. List them here and then X them out as a symbolic act of eliminating them. Now, forget about it and go to work!

Notes:

JOBS   *Success Factor 41*

Working Definition: The tasks we perform in our work or positions on an organization chart.

Success Factor: All jobs are important or they wouldn't exist. The tasks we perform in any job must be important and not menial. Effective managers insure that employees are working on the right things in their jobs.

Application: Treat all jobs as thought they are important—because they are!

(see Success Factor 19 for an application.)

Verses to Consider: Genesis 2:15; II Thessalonians 3:10

Being More Successful: Do I treat all jobs as though they are important? What have I overlooked?

To Do: Show your employees you value the job they do.

Notes:

Davis Woodruff, PE, CMC

JUSTICE   *Success Factor 42*

Working Definition: Getting what is deserved in the way of consequences when work rules, accepted practices or policies are not followed.

Success Factor: Managers will maintain discipline and order in the work group by insuring fair and equitable treatment for each employee. Work rules, practices and policies are to be enforced consistently and fairly for all. Now, sometimes one may practice mercy instead of justice, but that is generally an exception based on some extenuating circumstance and should be clearly documented for future reference.

Application: One must consciously work at being fair, consistent and just in dealing with people issues.

Verse to Consider: Amos 5:24

Being More Successful: Can you identify any situations of unequal treatment (consequences) or perceived unequal treatment in your organization? What about favoritism?

To Do: Make a list of specific policies or rules that you deal with routinely and note what steps you will take when the desired behavior or results are not seen. Stick to it no matter who is involved.

Notes:

KEEP *Success Factor 43*

Working Definition: The stuff you hang on to, whether it be tangible or intangible, such as relationships.

Success Factor: The successful manager will know what he or she should keep and what they should let go. Sometimes, it is more important to sacrifice short term gains in order to keep the long term focus. For example, an employee may be going through difficult times that prevent them from maintaining the expected performance levels. Instead of letting them go, you decide to keep them and help them get through the issue. In which case, you'll have a loyal employee later. Now, about stuff. Keep records according to your records retention plan and get rid of what's outdated.

Application: Know what you need to keep and what you need to let go.

Verse to Consider: II Timothy 4:5

Being More Successful: Which employees will you work to keep even in the face of difficulties? Which can you easily let go? What records are essential to you and how long should they be kept? Which relationships with customers matter the most to you? Are there some customers or suppliers you don't need to keep?

To Do: Evaluate whether you are keeping the right stuff.

Notes:

KINDNESS

Success Factor 44

Working Definition: Treating people like you want to be treated. Respecting individuals in the work place.

Success Factor: Until an employee demonstrates they won't accept kindness, the effective manager will treat all employees with kindness. Even then kindness should rule our actions.

Application: In a world filled with violence, hate and corruption take time to demonstrate kindness to each employee. You'll be repaid many times over.

Verse to Consider: Ephesians 4:32

Being More Successful: What can I do to show more kindness to my employees? (This does not have to cost money, but rather is how you deal with people and what you do to help them do their jobs.)

To Do: Find specific ways you can show kindness in your workplace.

Notes:

LEADERSHIP   *Success Factor 45*

Working Definition: Providing a work environment that gets people to do what needs to be done because they want to do it.

Success Factor: While there are different styles of leadership, all leaders are responsible for getting results through the efforts of other people. Effective managers realize you lead people, but manage processes and things.

Application: Leadership is driven by example. Good performance in employees is a function of what they see in their leader. You are in a leadership position if you are a manager or supervisor the issue is what kind of leader you are?

Verses to Consider: Genesis 33:13-16; Exodus 15:13; Nehemiah 2:17-18; Philippians 2:13-14

Being More Successful: Have you been aware of those leadership behaviors that may negatively affect the people who report to you?

To Do: What changes should you make in your leadership behaviors that will have a positive impact in your workplace?

Notes:

Davis Woodruff, PE, CMC

LEARN *Success Factor 46*

Working Definition: Grasping new ideas and principles, especially in the areas of human relations and technology.

Success Factor: The work place is changing rapidly and constantly driven by costs and competition. Effective managers respond, adapt to and become pro-active by learning new skills and information.

Application: Look for opportunities to learn. Don't avoid learning new skills and techniques and technologies. Be willing to grasp new ideas and approaches.

Verses to Consider: Proverbs 23:12; II Timothy 2:15

Being More Successful: What do you need to learn this week? This month? This year?

To Do: Make an effort learn new stuff that will affect how you work and how you work with your people. Read technical journals or management materials each week and apply what you learn. A good management text, perhaps the best ever written, is the Holy Bible. Read it every day.

Notes:

LEAVE

Success Factor 47

Working Definition: To go away from a business, place, situation, relationship or job.

Success Factor: There are times in a career when one knows it is time to leave; whether it is a particular position in a company or even going to a new company. Knowing when to leave is the difficult part of the equation, but you know you know when you know you know.

Application: When you disagree with over 51% of the decisions made within the organization, it's probably time to leave. When organizational decisions go against your personal core values, it may be time to leave.

Verse to Consider: Ecclesiastes 3:1

Being More Successful: Are there decisions being made with which you disagree? Are these related to values and real issues, or just something you don't like?

To Do: Make plans for your next career steps, whether in your present company or with another.

Notes:

LISTEN   *Success Factor 48*

Working Definition: To really hear what someone is telling you, whether it involves the words, the emotions or the body language.

Success Factor: Employees want managers who will really listen. To listen means that first you must stop talking and focus on the other person. Concentrate on what they're telling you and quit thinking about what you'll say next. Oh yes, get rid of distractions and really focus. When the manager really listens, they earn the respect of their employees.

Application: Make a conscious effort to be a better listener and focus on the other person.

Verse to Consider: James 1:19

Being More Successful: What are your barriers to listening? (i.e., time, distractions, don't care). I once had a boss who always allowed the phone to interrupt our conversations. After a few times of this happening, I would simply get up and leave his office when he answered the phone during a conversation with me. Of course, I didn't return until he came looking for me. It only took a couple of times before he asked what I was doing. When I explained it, he realized the message he had been sending to me, that what we were discussing was less important than whatever the phone call would be about. We both learned a valuable lesson about listening and getting rid of distractions!

To Do: Work to improve your listening skills. Find a course on listening and schedule a date for it. At the very least list how you will improve your listening skills within the next month.

Notes:

MANAGEMENT   *Success Factor 49*

Working Definition: Actions taken to plan, staff, organize, delegate and control in order to get the work done.

Success Factor: Management relates to processes, products and procedures, not people. We lead people. Effective managers will make sure the work is planned, proper staffing is available, the work is organized, properly delegated and controlled.

Application: The most important part of management is planning. It's a great myth that managers like to plan and are good planners. Blast the myth, actually become an effective planner which will make you a better manager.

Verse to Consider: Proverbs 20:18

Being More Successful: What are you doing to plan, staff, organize, delegate and control the work being done? What should you be doing better?

To Do: Make a chart of the five functions of management and how each relates specifically to your job. Use this as a guide to help you plan how you will spend your time.

Notes:

MEASUREMENT *Success Factor 50*

Working Definition: Evaluating results; using numbers to determine where we stand relative to a target or goal.

Success Factor: It has been said that if we can't measure it, don't do it. Identify those five to seven critical factors that tell us the health of our organization or work group. Know the units we will use to describe performance, for example: # work orders completed in a shift; labor hours/work order; good pounds per day; # good parts/shift; lbs. of waste/shift; # loads/day; mpg; # of students sent to detention; grade distributions; environmental incidents; safety incidents; etc. Next, set targets and evaluate performance using the data and information from the process

Application: Too often we look at situations subjectively and make decisions based upon emotions and supposition instead of measuring and evaluating performance using real data.

Verses to Consider: Amos 7:7-9

Being More Successful: What are the five to seven factors critical to your unit's success?

To Do: Take your list and identify the units of measure, the frequency of measurement, the communications of the results and the corrective actions when you fail to meet the desired target.

Notes:

MONEY *Success Factor 51*

Working Definition: What we work to earn as individuals and businesses. Also, the stuff that "the love of is the root of all evil."

Success Factor: Businesses must earn money—make a profit to stay in business. Effective managers understand this principle, but apply it with integrity. The same must be true for individuals and families.

Application: A little gained honestly is better than a lot that cost your integrity.

Verses to Consider: Proverbs 11:1; Ecclesiastes 5:10; I Timothy 6:10; Hebrews 13:5

Being More Successful: Are we making a reasonable profit, or are we taking advantage of our customers? What can we do to improve profits without raising prices?

To Do: List several immediate action steps you can take to improve profits.

Notes:

MOTIVATION *Success Factor 52*

Working Definition: The "want to" for getting the job done on time and correctly.

Success Factor: There are two extremes when it comes to motivation: you can motivate anyone to do anything or you cannot motivate another person they must motivate themselves. The truth is somewhere between these extremes. The manager sets the climate for people doing their jobs on time and correctly. By listening, paying attention to details, getting to know your people and above all, being fair and honest with each one the manager can establish a positive work environment that leads to motivated employees. Appreciation for a job well done is a powerful motivator. Just saying "thanks" can do wonders. Remember the old saying, "you can lead a horse to water, but you can't make him drink." But, you can put salt in his food!

Application: Look for ways to set a positive work environment that leads to motivated employees. Listen to your people and treat each one with dignity and respect while being honest and fair in all your dealings.

Verse to Consider: Proverbs 16:2

Being More Successful: What are the things you do to enable your people to have the "want to"? What things do you do to discourage your people?

To Do: Make it a point today to listen to your people and to tell them thank you for what they're doing.

Notes:

NEGLECT   *Success Factor 53*

Working Definition: Not paying attention to something or someone who needs attention.

Success Factor: When you see something that needs correcting it is your responsibility to either do it or get it done. For example, high scrap rates in a process cannot be overlooked. Neither can you overlook the cleanliness of work areas or the weeds in the parking lot. All of these are details that cannot be neglected by the effective manager. Even more important is being sure that you do not neglect your employees. Sometimes a particular employee may get overlooked when people are being recognized. The janitor, person doing the yard maintenance, librarian, mechanic, driver, mail clerk or whomever is considered to have the least significant job in your organization often get overlooked. Make it a point to notice these members of your team. It will make your day and their day! It will also help with motivation (see #52).

Application: Know what cannot be overlooked or neglected in your business.

Verses to Consider: Joshua 1:8; Proverbs 3:1-2

Being More Successful: What are three areas that are easy for you to overlook? What jobs are often considered the "least noticeable" in your organization?

To Do: Take action on each of the items you listed above.

Notes:

Davis Woodruff, PE, CMC

NEVER'S *Success Factor 54*

Working Definition: Behaviors that are not allowed in the work place.

Success Factor: Successful managers NEVER: 1) compromise their integrity; 2) discipline an employee in public; 3) allow a safety or regulatory concern to go uncorrected; or 4) fail to serve customers.

Application: While others may do things differently, practicing these "four never's" will help you succeed as a manager.

Verses to Consider: Proverbs 3:25-26

Being More Successful: Am I guilty of violating these four never's? What amends need to be made, if any? Do we have known safety or other regulatory issues that need attention?

To Do: Make yourself a table or chart of the "4 Never's" and how they specifically apply to you and your job.

Notes:

New

Success Factor 55

Working Definition: Generally, anything that is being changed is considered "new."

Success Factor: Managing change is critical for managers today. Realizing that folks will not always readily accept the "new" and taking steps to preclude and overcome objections will make the new ways stick. Of course, this means planning when bringing in the "new." Whether people, processes, products, facilities or infrastructure are the "new"; planning and communicating are musts for success.

Application: When you fail to plan and communicate to all involved it is not likely that you will be successful in implementing something "new" into your business. Thus, to be successful the manager must plan and communicate. Both of these take TIME.

Verses to Consider: Revelation 21:1-5

Being More Successful: What are four or five "new" items that are on the agenda for your business during the next six months?

To Do: List the plans for bringing in the new. Include tasks, dates, responsibilities, expected results and communications.

Notes:

Davis Woodruff, PE, CMC

NOTICE
Success Factor 56

Working Definition: The art of carefully observing and "paying attention" to an employee or work performance.

Success Factor: In today's fast paced and impersonal world, an effective manager will make the effort to notice each employee and recognize their contribution.

Application: Work is about 80% social and a great part of it is the attention given to and received from fellow workers.

Verse to Consider: Acts 4:13

Being More Successful: Do you notice the details in the work place? Do you pay attention to each employee each day? Do you monitor and notice work performance?

To Do: Really notice your employees and the work they do. Let them know that you know their contribution to the organization.

Notes:

Observe

Success Factor 57

Working Definition: To be completely aware of all that's going on around you.

Success Factor: Effective manager's know the condition of all their resources: people, processes, facilities, infrastructure, equipment, and reserves.

Application: Make a list of each area of your business and identify the key observations you need to make in each.

Verses to Consider: I Corinthians 5:6-7

Being More Successful: Do you know what needs to be observed in your work area? Don't forget safety and compliance issues. For sure, observe security needs in today's world!

To Do: List several immediate action steps you can take to really observe what's going on around you. Begin with a list of observations as suggested above.

Notes:

Davis Woodruff, PE, CMC

Once
Success Factor 58

Working Definition: Once is the only opportunity you have to make a good first impression on a customer (or anyone else for that matter); once is the only chance you have for a fresh start with a new employee.

Success Factor: Realize the importance of those "once" or one-time events in your business. Plan for them and make the most of them for the future of your organization. During the first three days on the job is when the new employee will form opinions and attitudes that will be with them for as long as they work for you. Make it positive!

Application: Identify the "once" events coming up in your business and plan to make them successful.

Verses to Consider: Hebrews 9:27-28

Being More Successful: List the "once" events with employees, customers or others that will occur within the next few months in your business.

To Do: Plan for these events, include the expected outcomes.

Notes:

☐RGANIZING   *Success Factor 59*

Working Definition: Organizing is one of the functions of management described in Success Factor #49. Arranging and performing work and work processes in an orderly manner.

Success Factor: The effective manager realizes the importance of an orderly approach in work and in processes while making delegation of work a reality.

Application: All work should be done in a planned and organized manner to experience maximum productivity from people and processes.

Verses to Consider: Nehemiah 4:13-20

Being More Successful: Is the work being done by my employees organized so as to prevent wasted time and effort? Are processes organized properly to insure optimum material flow?

To Do: Flow chart the work processes in your area of responsibility and look for ways to simplify or better organize the work being done.

Notes:

OVERKILL

Success Factor 60

Working Definition: What we tend to do with little problems that can be solved easily while ignoring the bigger issues that need real root cause analysis and corrective actions.

Success Factor: When problems or issues arise it is vital that managers recognize the severity and nature of the real problem. When it can affect people, processes, products, customers or compliance the problem must be dealt with in an appropriate manner. Too often we take a simple issue and over complicate it or implement overkill procedures that stifle productivity and motivation. For example, when employees are abusing cell phones we institute a no cell phone policy rather than dealing with the abuse.

Application: Effective managers will know what problems need real solutions and recognize when the deadly menace of "overkill" is beginning to cloud their thinking.

Verse to Consider: I Samuel 17:38-40

Being More Successful: Can you identify a few issues where "overkill" tactics have been employed?

To Do: Now, let's eliminate at least one of the "overkill" procedures we've put in place at some point.

Notes:

Taking Care of the Basics

Performance   *Success Factor 61*

Working Definition: How people do their work and how well processes produce outputs.

Success Factor: Performance requirements should be defined for each employee and for each process (see Measurement, #50).

Application: For each employee who reports to you, the performance criteria should be established and communicated to each employee. For each of your critical processes performance criteria should be defined. What are they? Well, maybe you are responsible for the sales force. Would valid performance criteria be the number of sales calls or the number of actual sales or the sales dollars? The successful manager will identify and define the most appropriate performance criteria. Sounds a lot like expectations, doesn't it?

Verses to Consider: Proverbs 5:21; Proverbs 12:11; Proverbs 13:4; Matthew 16:27

Being More Successful: List your employees and processes. Now, define the performance criteria.

To Do: Communicate the performance criteria to each employee and to each supervisor or process team leader.

Notes:

PLANNING

Success Factor 62

Working Definition: The process of analyzing situations, identifying options, considering alternatives, determining what will be done, by whom and when.

Success Factor: The cost effective manager is an effective planner. With the cost and competitive pressures of today, planning is more critical than ever before in business. In some organizations products or services are produced by dedicated people and "brute force" rather than through planned and efficient processes. Successful organizations break out of this trap and focus on planning.

Application: Plans should be as specific as possible. The details of what is to be done, by whom and when are all vital to achieving your objectives. But even more important is executing your plan!

Verse to Consider: Proverbs 16:3

Being More Successful: Do I have up to date plans to achieve my objectives?

To Do: Identify the steps you can take to improve your planning process. Implement your plans. Follow-up!

Notes:

PREPARATION   *Success Factor 63*

Working Definition: Planning and actions taken to insure success before the work is actually done.

Success Factor: Most managers today are so busy on administrative and other details that proper preparation and planning go lacking in many cases. In the "get it done now" or instant society in which we live and work, it's difficult to step back and take some time to think (cogitate) upon an idea, situation or work to be done. Thus, we often charge ahead without thinking of the alternatives or consequences that are a part of good preparation.

Application: Know when it's time to step back and properly prepare to do the work assigned to you and your organization. When new equipment comes in, don't be in such a rush to start it up that you forget about the maintenance procedures or safety issues before start up. When new people come into your organization take time before they arrive to prepare for their first three days on the job. Make these days positive, productive and beneficial for you and the employee.

Verse to Consider: Matthew 24:44

Being More Successful: Recognize those areas where you often overlook proper preparation. Write them down:

To Do: For at least one of the areas you listed above make the plans to be properly prepared to insure success in the future.

Notes:

Davis Woodruff, PE, CMC

PROCEDURES *Success Factor 64*

Working Definition: Simple documents that describe the work to be done and how to do it. Documents that provide for consistency among employees.

Success Factor: Up to date procedures are needed for every process and job in your organization. Work procedures are best written by the people actually doing the work. Procedures must be controlled in such a manner as to prevent using obsolete ones.

Application: Allow employees to be involved in preparing procedures. After the procedures are implemented, life is simpler for managers and employees.

Verses to Consider: Exodus 16:16-20

Being More Successful: Are documented procedures needed in your work place? Do our procedures need improvements?

To Do: Review procedures in your work area and insure they are up to date and relevant. Look for barriers to getting the work done that may be buried in some of your procedures.

Notes:

Processes *Success Factor 65*

Working Definition: The sets of events working together to produce an outcome. Processes have inputs, output and ideally have controls or control points that are specified.

Success Factor: Managers are often focused on procedures and administrative tasks and fail to take an overall process management approach. When we become focused on the details of various tasks we often overlook the larger issues associated with the processes we manage. Remember, processes are not just making stuff, but can be as varied as data input, testing, maintenance, internal quality audits, environmental systems, etc. We need to identify the peripheral or support processes as well as the actual manufacturing or service processes.

Application: It's time to use one of the tools of management. Simple flow charts like this one will help you identify your processes:

> **Inputs:→Process:→Outputs:**
>
> **Controls:**

Verses to Consider: Nehemiah 2:1-9; Ephesians 2:8-9

Being More Successful: For what processes are you responsible? What are the inputs, outputs and controls?

To Do: Flow chart your work processes. Focus on inputs, outputs and controls. Where controls are lacking, identify and implement control points.

Notes:

Davis Woodruff, PE, CMC

QUALITY  *Success Factor 66*

Working Definition: Whatever the customer says it is! At a minimum quality is meeting the expectations of the customer.

Success Factor: The struggle for quality never ends. It requires constant attention to detail, communication of requirements throughout the organization and measuring results through quality objectives.

Application: Effective managers make quality a demonstrated priority along with safety, production and regulatory concerns.

Verses to Consider: Genesis 1:10; 21

Being More Successful: How do we know and measure quality in our business?

To Do: Be sure you know the requirements for quality in your operations or business. Clearly communicate these requirements to each employee. If you've already done this, now would be a good time to review it in detail with your people.

Notes:

QUANDARIES   *Success Factor 67*

Working Definition: The situation many managers find themselves in when they fail to plan properly or to consider alternatives. During these times the work force is waiting for you to make a decision.

Success Factor: When you find yourself in a difficult situation take a long look at it from all angles, try to look at your options or alternatives and select the one that will yield the most effective results in the short term and in the long term. Realize the importance of prevention by planning ahead!

Application: In business we need to think of those areas that give us the most "trouble." Sometimes they are the overlooked areas or areas driven by external factors. Know which factors need to be considered before you get into what could be called a "mess" with many diverse issues involved.

Verses to Consider: Ecclesiastes 2:11

Being More Successful: What are some recent "quandaries" you've encountered? How could they have been prevented?

To Do: Identify at least one situation and the necessary steps you can take to prevent a "mess."

Notes:

Davis Woodruff, PE, CMC

QUESTIONS   *Success Factor 68*

Working Definition: Those items for which employees need an exact answer.

Success Factor: Effective managers encourage questions from employees and customers and provide timely accurate answers. When managers don't encourage questions, employees often do their work in ignorance and make costly mistakes.

Application: Invite questions by your actions and words as a manager. It's okay not to have an immediate answer. Don't make up answers, simply say "I don't know, but will find out and get back to you." Then do it! An employee's or customer's question deserves a timely and accurate response.

Verses to Consider: Matthew 16:15-17

Being More Successful: How do I encourage or discourage questions? Do I get timely and accurate answers for my employees?

To Do: Encourage questions in your workplace by your behavior and by talking with each employee frequently.

Notes:

Taking Care of the Basics

REGULATIONS *Success Factor 69*

Working Definition: Externally imposed requirements, generally by a local, state or federal law or agency. Regulatory compliance is a MUST for doing business.

Success Factor: Know the regulatory requirements that are applicable to your operations. Regulatory compliance is not optional. It must take equal priority with production, safety and quality. In some cases it may take a higher priority.

Application: Establish and implement a process for staying up to date with the regulatory requirements that affect your operation. Identify the legal and regulatory requirements with which you must comply. These may include DOT, OSHA, EPA, FAA, FDA, EEOC, or a myriad of others.

Verse to Consider: Matthew 28:19-20

Being More Successful: Educate yourself and your people on the regulatory requirements that must be satisfied. Emphasize the importance of compliance. Implement a process for routine compliance reviews done by knowledgeable personnel within your organization.

To Do: List the regulatory requirements that apply to your operations and then review to be sure you are in compliance. Keep this list up to date. Insure that you have a procedure in place to maintain up to date requirements and compliance reviews.

Notes:

Reinforcement — *Success Factor 70*

Working Definition: Positive or negative performance feedback provided to an employee.

Success Factor: Positive reinforcement has been proven to be far more effective than negative reinforcement (punishment) for improving performance or changing behavior. Effective leaders reinforce desired behaviors and provide negative reinforcement to eliminate or change undesirable behaviors in the work place.

Application: Be sure people know what is expected. Make a consistent effort to reinforce your people. Look for opportunities to say "thank you" for a job well done. Consider mailing letters home when something special has been accomplished at work. This will involve the family in the positive reinforcement, because most of the time the family only hears the negative stuff about work.

Verses to Consider: Romans 2:6; 2 Corinthians 5:10

Being More Successful: There is an old rule in performance management which says managers should provide about four times as much positive reinforcement as punishment. Look for someone doing something that deserves reinforcement and then simply say "thank you" or "good job." Do it everyday.

To Do: Get started today with a consistent and conscious effort to provide positive reinforcement for each of your employees. At the same time identify those situations where negative reinforcement is necessary and get busy on those. It may help you to keep a log of your efforts to remind you of what you're actually accomplishing. This may serve as to reinforce you. Don't forget to reinforce your bosses, they're people too!

Notes:

Relationships — *Success Factor 71*

Working Definition: The association or companionship of two or more people in the work place. Realize that people in organizations generally care about each other.

Success Factor: Relationships are built on trust. Good relationships are the path to success for effective managers. Effective managers know that ultimately the work of the organization is accomplished by people working together. Good relationships among employees are critical to having a productive work place. Many managers spend too much time on administrative stuff and/or production concerns and too little time building relationships.

Application: Studies have shown that 80% of the failures in the work place are the result of poor relationships. To be effective managers must work at building solid relationships based on mutual respect and trust. Leadership is all about relationships with people

Verses to Consider: Matthew 24:4-5

Being More Successful: How are your relationships with your employees? With other departments or business units? Among your employees? Be aware of "baggage" in relationships. You may not know what happened before you came on the scene. Sometimes people will have "axes to grind" at the expense of the organization.

To Do: Work daily to build better relationships in the workplace.

Notes:

Resources *Success Factor 72*

Working Definition: The people, equipment, facilities, money, materials and infrastructure required to get the work done or products produced for your customers.

Success Factor: Effective use of resources is a constant challenge in today's work place. It is one of the "make or break" areas for managers. Resource utilization can be the difference in profit and loss; or in high turnover and low turnover. Know what resources are required and what resources are available to you.

Application: List all the business and/or manufacturing processes in your areas of responsibility. Identify the resource requirements for each process. Develop and implement a plan for more effective resource utilization. Write out your plan and follow it. By the way, this can be a great tool for communicating with your managers and for justifying or explaining your needs to top management.

Verses to Consider: Luke 14:28-33

Being More Successful: Look for opportunities to improve resource utilization and for developing your people. For example, energy conservation can return significant dividends in many businesses. In one case with which I am very familiar, an organization saved nearly $100,000 per year from improved steam trap maintenance in processing areas. Sometimes the seemingly "little things" pay huge returns!

To Do: Identify the resource requirements, availability and improvement opportunities in your operations. In most cases this could involve identifying improved competencies needed by the people in your organization.

Notes:

RESPECT   *Success Factor 73*

Working Definition: The attitude employees develop towards their leaders based upon the qualities and actions of the leader. Respecting someone is different from liking someone.

Success Factor: Effective managers will work every day to earn the respect and trust of their employees. Respect is earned by the actions you take every day in the little things as well as in the big things. People will respect a manager who is honest, hard working, respects them, treats people with dignity, makes the tough decisions and sticks by them, and who supports his people. Respect is earned not freely given.

Application: Manage everyday in a way that will earn the respect of your employees, customers, suppliers and all with whom you come in contact. Being respect is far more valuable than being liked. It's not easy to do it right, but it's the only way that will yield long term and lasting results for the manager.

Verses to Consider: Titus 3:1-2

Being More Successful: Early in my career I managed a department of skilled folks. This department was an administrative nightmare and the people did not trust nor respect their previous manager. Each day I worked at building relationships based upon mutual respect and trust. Many of the people did not like me because of the decisions that had to be made and the changes that had to be implemented. Years later several of these people came to me and told me that while they may not have liked me or the things I did in the department they respected me as a leader. They said, "you told us like it was and treated us fairly and right." What more could a manager ask?

To Do: Treat people with dignity and respect, be honest with them, and be consistent to earn their respect. Everyday work to build respect and trust.

Notes:

Resolve

Success Factor 74

Working Definition: Resolve is the ability to make a decision and stick by it; or to set a direction for the business and "stay the course."

Success Factor: Making decisions is difficult, but sticking by them is even more difficult. Many times managers make choices or implement changes that are difficult but necessary. Then, when a few folks get upset they change again or back off the new ways. Sometimes that can be a good thing, but most of the time it simple demonstrates a lack of resolve by the manager. You can't please everyone, so resolve to "stay the course' once you've set the direction.

Application: When making difficult decisions or implementing change use a process based on facts and you will be more confident of your actions. Your confidence will be evident to your people and there will be more "buy-in." Once you implement a plan, stay the course unless new information indicates you should change it.

Verses to Consider: Proverbs 24:10; Revelation 2:2

Being More Successful: Be willing to make the tough choices and set the direction for your work group or business. Realize it will not be easy. Stick to it. Demonstrate your resolve.

To Do: When making decisions and charting a course for your organization, understand the situation and deal in facts. Then, be confident in what you do and stay the course.

Notes:

Results

Success Factor 75

Working Definition: The productive outcomes of work.

Success Factor: Results are not the same as activities. Effective managers focus on productive outcomes not on activities.

Application: Performance criteria and goals should be based on **results** to be achieved. Generally speaking the desired results will revolve around profits and customer satisfaction.

Verse to Consider: 2 Corinthians 5:10

Being More Successful: Do our goals or objectives focus on results? Do I measure performance based on results or activities? What do I need to change?

To Do: Identify the performance results you desire for each employee and communicate the results you expect to see.

Notes:

Davis Woodruff, PE, CMC

Serve

Success Factor 76

Working Definition: What managers should do for employees and customers.

Success Factor: One definition of management could be helping employees do their job by meeting their needs and serving the organization. If managers serve their employees instead of being aloof or arrogant the employees will usually respond by meeting or exceeding expectations and goals.

Application: Today, perhaps more than at any time in our history, folks need to be appreciated for what they do and have their need for "belonging" met by their supervisors. Look for ways to serve. For example, stay and help clean up the conference room after a meeting; pour the coffee during meetings; pick up paper in the parking lot; or, a myriad of other small tasks that will demonstrate to all who see that you are serious about serving. Sure these are small examples, but they illustrate the point quite well. Another personal example is in order here. Recently while conducting a series of management workshops for a client I helped the secretaries bring in the food and arrange the tables and chairs in the training facility. The people arriving noticed that the leader was willing to do what needed to be done. Now, when I call the secretary is always helpful; the people I work with respond more rapidly and provide more than I expect from them. It kind of goes back to the "Golden Rule."

Verses to Consider: Matthew 20:26-28

Being More Successful: Your success as a manager is ultimately determined by the success of your people. Thus, when you help meet their needs and help them succeed you are helping yourself and the organization be more successful. Another of those "paradoxes of management."

To Do: Think about how you go about a "routine" day at work. What are two or three simple things you could do that will demonstrate your commitment to serve?

Notes:

SINCERITY — *Success Factor 77*

Working Definition: Freedom from hypocrisy and fake intentions.

Success Factor: Employees deserve and expect sincerity in their dealings with their boss. This includes sincere praise, discipline and concern for their well-being.

Application: Employees can spot a faked interest "a mile away." Don't try to "fake it"—be real with your employees. You have probably seen managers who simply are not interested in people, but try to act like they are interested in what they have to say. In one case recently it was obvious the person was not really interested in my answers to questions, but they "acted like" they were interested. Many times I was tempted to answer the "wrong" question or say something off the wall to see if they were really sincere about the question they'd asked or the answer I gave!

Verse to Consider: Proverbs 15:2

Being More Successful: Have you been aware of times when you were not sincere with your employees? If so, what can you do to correct the situation?

To Do: List two or three actions that will demonstrate your sincerity to your employees. Now, follow through.

Notes:

Davis Woodruff, PE, CMC

Solutions   *Success Factor 78*

Working Definition: The answer(s) to the problems that must be solved in your operations, business systems or personnel situations.

Success Factor: It is important that you identify solutions and not just "point out" problems that need to be solved. Problem Pointers are a dime a dozen. Problem Solvers are very valuable to their organizations.

Application: When you are faced with a problem follow a logical process to find the solution. Define the problem carefully, collect the necessary data or information, do the proper analysis, determine the root cause, identify alternatives, choose the best solution, implement your solution and follow-up for effectiveness. If you are not fully responsible for implementing the solutions; at a minimum attempt to present your manager with a couple of alternatives to consider in arriving at the solution to be implemented.

Verses to Consider: Matthew 25:25-29

Being More Successful: Look for solutions, don't just identify problems. Problems without solutions are just more concerns for you, managers, employees or customers. When major problems or challenges arise in organizations and solutions are tough, remember that people will usually rise to meet a challenge.

To Do: Demonstrate initiative (#36) by taking on a couple of those "nagging" problems in your organization. Look for solutions and get on with solving them.

Notes:

Staffing

Working Definition: Selecting the right person for the right job. This is one of the five functions of management mentioned in Success Factor 49.

Success Factor: Effective managers use a selection process that enables them to choose the right person for the job. This process should include defining the required competencies for the position. Successful mangers and organizations make an effort to place people in positions where they can succeed. One of the most miserable (and unsuccessful) production managers I've seen was a very talented technical person who was put into production "to help his career" instead of being allowed to remain in the technical ranks. He was the proverbial "fish out of water" and ultimately the company lost a valuable contributor.

Application: A selection process that works: 1) Define the requirements of the job; 2) Identify the required competencies for the job; 3) Determine what you expect from someone in the job; 4) Use a selection profile; and 5) Clearly communicate with the candidate for the job.

Verses to Consider: Judges 7:4-9

Being More Successful: Do you have a well defined and organized process for staffing? If so, can it be improved? If not, what would one look like for your organization?

To Do: Think about two or three steps you can take to improve your staffing practices. These steps could involve things like using selection instruments, revising an interview process, or having more than one person interview candidates.

Notes:

TEACH

Success Factor 80

Working Definition: To impart knowledge and experiences to employees that will help them be more successful on their job and to develop them for the future.

Success Factor: Most managers have a lot of what Dr. W. Edwards Deming called "profound knowledge." This is often called "institutional knowledge" which is knowledge of the organization, relationships, processes, production issues, problems that have been solved, customer information, etc. that needs to be passed along to the mangers of the future.

Application: Managers need to take advantage of opportunities to teach employees those things that will help them be more effective or successful now and in the future. This is different from the more formal or classroom type training. It's sort of like mentoring with a focus on helping people learn information that perhaps only you could impart to them.

Verse to Consider: Isaiah 28:26

Being More Successful: Take time to reflect on your career. Make notes for yourself about the events, people, problems, issues, products, customers, employees, relationships or other items of interest in your organization. Jot down a few words or sentences on these topics and use them to help you remember what to teach your employees. They need to learn from your experiences. Successful managers develop people for the future.

To Do: Make a conscious effort to teach the employees of today that will become the managers of tomorrow. You will be helping others, yourself and your organization.

Notes:

TECHNOLOGY *Success Factor 81*

Working Definition: Science applied to the work place. Often thought of in terms of electronic stuff like computers and e-mail, but much more inclusive than just electronics.

Success Factor: Using technology wisely requires managers to stay abreast of the latest trends in their industry or business. Technology is a tool not an end in itself.

Application: Don't become so enamored with technology that you lose sight of your real goals. Always take care of the basics with your people and let technology be a tool to help you.

Verse to Consider: Isaiah 54:2

Being More Successful: How are we using technology more effectively today than two years ago in our business? What new technologies do we need? Don't forget process requirements, pollution prevention or productivity improvement technology applications.

To Do: Identify technology needs and applications and even overuse and do something about it.

Notes:

Davis Woodruff, PE, CMC

TERMINATION — *Success Factor 82*

Working Definition: Removing an employee from their job due to performance or other issues.

Success Factor: Termination usually represents failure by the employee, manager, a previous manager, the organization or perhaps all of these. Termination in business is kind of like capital punishment in society; it is the ultimate and should be rarely and carefully used. There should be no surprises when terminations occur. Performance issues should have been documented and clearly communicated to the employee while opportunities to correct the problems or situations are provided. For those offenses that may require immediate termination there should still be no surprises, because they should have been clearly documented and communicated in an employee manual or similar document. During my career I've had supervisors come in and say something like "we've got to fire so-and-so." When asked why, the answer would be something like "they're not doing their job." Sadly, when the files would be reviewed the last performance appraisal was very good and not issues had been documented since. At that point the conversation usually turned to the fact that somewhere in all of this the supervisor had failed to do their job!

Application: Be sure you understand the offenses in your employee guidelines that are grounds for immediate termination. If you are dealing with performance issues, it is essential that you document and communicate. Keep good records. Have them reviewed by your manager or follow another process that has been defined for your organization.

Verse to Consider: Luke 12:48

Being More Successful: If you ever have to terminate an employee, prepare in advance with a written statement that sticks to the issues at hand. Have another person present. State the purpose of the meeting, read your prepared statement and have the person leave immediately. Do not "ad lib" or get into a discussion. Those conversations should have been held months ago in most cases.

To Do: Learn what your employee handbook says about termination and the process your business uses. If you don't have written guidelines, there's no time like now to write them.

Notes:

TIME   *Success Factor 83*

Working Definition: The stuff of which there's never enough! i.e. 24 hours per day or $$$$.

Success Factor: Effective managers are aware of time and manage themselves with respect for the clock. They also are careful to avoid wasting the time of their employees. Most people consider meetings a waste of time and negative, yet we continue to over schedule meetings. Expect delays in projects when dealing with external and internal parties. Plan your time allocation each day, but realize the plan will probably change!

Application: Plan your days and weeks and follow your plans. Sure, they'll change, but without plans you'll never effectively manage yourself. By the way, are you wasting time on the internet? Spend your time on productive tasks, don't waste valuable time on "grandiose" plans that will not be implemented. Don't spend your time managing history and writing voluminous reports, just record what's needed and move on.

Verses to Consider: Psalm 39:4; Ecclesiastes 3:1,11

Being More Successful: Do I know "where my time goes?" What about my employees? Am I wasting the time of my employees? Are meetings productive?

To Do: Analyze where your time goes. Come up with several ways to improve your time utilization. For example, maybe you can eliminate one meeting or conference call per week. A savings like that is multiplied over the course of a year.

Notes:

UNDERSTANDING — *Success Factor 84*

Working Definition: Knowing and being familiar with particular situations, processes, people, equipment or jobs.

Success Factor: It's easy to understand processes and equipment. Effective managers take the time and make the effort to really understand their employees.

Application: Spending time with each employee and listening to them will help your understanding of "why they do what they do."

Verses to Consider: Proverbs 1:33; 4:11

Being More Successful: How well do I understand what is expected of me? How well do I understand the processes and products in my area? Now, what about my understanding of the people?

To Do: Look for ways to focus on your people and improve your understanding of your employees.

Notes:

Davis Woodruff, PE, CMC

UNCERTAINTY — *Success Factor 85*

Working Definition: The lack of predictability in our businesses, processes, relationships or economy. Since September 11, 2001 the level of uncertainty has increased for all of us in every area of life.

Success Factor: Effective managers recognize that uncertainty exists in all situations and take steps to manage that uncertainty wherever possible. This is best done through knowledge and understanding.

Application: Don't be paralyzed by uncertainty. Let it make you a better informed person and manager.

Verses to Consider: Proverbs 3:25-26

Being More Successful: How has the level of uncertainty changed in the past year in our business? What uncertainties concern me the most? What concerns my employees the most?

To Do: Identify your most glaring uncertainties and determine what you can do about them.

Notes:

VALUES   *Success Factor 86*

Working Definition: The absolutes we live by.

Success Factor: Truth, honesty, integrity, importance and worth of each individual, doing what's right are all values that are embraced by effective managers.

Application: Evaluate every situation and simply be guided by doing "what's right." When you aren't sure of what's right sometimes doing nothing is the right thing until you are sure.

Verses to Consider: Exodus 20:1-17

Being More Successful: What are my core values that do not change? What do I consider absolutes for life and in the work place?

To Do: Know your values and how they relate to your job. What do I need to change or NOT change? Communicate your values to those in your organization.

Notes:

VARIATION *Success Factor 87*

Working Definition: The difference in things that should be the same.

Success Factor: Effective managers learn to use simple tools to identify, manage and reduce variation. Procedures can help in this process.

Application: Variation is always present—people, processes, methods, environment, products, literally everywhere! Using Statistical Process Control (SPC) and other simple techniques can help you manage variation, but before you begin using it see Success Factor #36!

Verse to Consider: Psalm 119:18

Being More Successful: Do you know the types and amount of variation present in your processes and products? What do you need to learn in order to use simple statistical methods?

To Do: Learn what you need to do in order to quantify variation in the processes and products in your work place. Next, work to reduce the variation in your processes and products.

Notes:

Vision — *Success Factor 88*

Working Definition: Looking ahead and seeing the things others don't see; and providing a long term sense of direction for the organization.

Success Factor: Spend time to look beyond today. Look ahead five or ten years and make your best estimate of what needs to happen in your business to continue being successful. Setting the vision and clearly communicating it to the organization is one of the two most important functions of leadership. (The other one is establishing and communicating the values.)

Application: Vision sets the overall direction for the organization and gives the people something to "hitch their wagon to." Vision needs to be relevant and practical, yet challenging for the organization to really embrace it.

Verse to Consider: Acts 2:17

Being More Successful: What is your vision for your organization? Is it clearly articulated to all members of the organization?

To Do: In ten words or less write your vision for your organization. Now, communicate it to the people.

Notes:

Davis Woodruff, PE, CMC

WASTE *Success Factor 89*

Working Definition: Anything that doesn't add value to your products or services.

Success Factor: Waste generally falls into one of six categories: 1) Waiting; 2) Damaged goods; 3) Doing things over (rework); 4) Performance barriers; 5) Dis-satisfied employees; 6) Dis-satisfied customers.

Application: Identify and categorize waste in your organization, then develop an action plan to eliminate it.

Verse to Consider: Proverbs 21:20

Being More Successful: How can we eliminate waste, not just control waste?

To Do: Identify the types and quantities of waste in your organization and how you can eliminate it. Be vigilant about eliminating waste. View it as $$$ lying around to be picked up and saved.

Notes:

WILLINGNESS — *Success Factor 90*

Working Definition: The desire to get the job done regardless of "whose job it is." Willingness is a first cousin to initiative

Success Factor: The desire to get a job done, no matter "whose it is" separates the effective and successful manager from the "average" manager. Reaching out to do work beyond your immediate area of responsibility will help you learn other areas of your business or organization while allowing you to demonstrate your desire to see the entire operation succeed.

Application: Look for areas where you can reach out and show your willingness to see the business succeed. Do more than is required or expected.

Verse to Consider: Proverbs 13:4

Being More Successful: Willingness is a success factor that is sadly in short supply in many organizations today. Willingness to seek more responsibility, accept responsibility, take calculated risks, make decisions and move beyond the minimum requirements of the job while not becoming "political animals" or "turf kings" is needed more than ever in business today.

To Do: Look for opportunities to demonstrate your willingness to get the job done. Your people and your bosses will recognize and appreciate what you're doing.

Notes:

Wisdom _____   *Success Factor 91*

Working Definition: Applied knowledge.

Success Factor: Many times we know more than we do. We know the importance of positive reinforcement, yet we fail to say thank you for a job well done. We understand the need to define and communicate expectations, yet we overlook this critical task. You get the point.

Application: Act wisely, apply what you KNOW. Many times it's not more knowledge that's needed, it's the wisdom to do something with the knowledge we already have.

Verses to Consider: Proverbs 2:6, Proverbs 17:24, Ecclesiastes 8:2

Being More Successful: Write out the things you KNOW that you should be doing, but are not doing as well as you should. Perhaps it's to use more positive reinforcement, or to deal with an issue that will require punishment, or to define and communicate expectations or to identify improvement opportunities for your people.

To Do: Apply what you know.

Notes:

WORK   *Success Factor 92*

Working Definition: Work is simply a task or tasks that must be accomplished.

Success Factor: Too often in business, employees don't really know what must be accomplished. Management has a responsibility to clearly define and communicate the work to be done.

Application: In every job and every process, effective managers will clearly define "the work to be done."

Verses to Consider: Genesis 2:15; Colossians 3:17

Being More Successful: In my work place is all work to be done clearly defined and communicated to the employees?

To Do: Define and communicate the work to be done.

Notes:

eXceptions

Success Factor 93

Working Definition: A work rule or procedure is knowingly violated in the interest of an employee, customer or business need.

Success Factor: While it's important to follow work rules and procedures, there are times in the real world when work rules or procedures may restrict a manager from acting in the best interest of an employee, customer or the business. Wisdom dictates that managers realize these unusual situations for what they are and make rare exceptions. A simple example may be in order here. There is a case where a single Mom with two children, one of whom is undergoing cancer treatments is being provided a house through an organization that builds houses for those in need. This Mom is trying to care for her kids and work to make ends meet. Yet, procedures and rules require that she put in a certain number of volunteer hours before she moves in. It may be a physical impossibility and is certainly stressful to her. Why not realize the complexity of the situation and simply require the hours be put in after she moves in and after the child finishes the treatments? Perhaps this is too simple. You get the idea. We frequently do things similar to this in the work place.

Application: Whenever exceptions are made to work rules or procedures, it requires legitimate justification. The problem, of course, is for the manager to recognize the situation and be willing to take a calculated risk. When an exception is made, the situation should be carefully documented and clearly communicated to all interested parties.

Verse to Consider: Matthew 24:35

Being More Successful: Exceptions that are not legitimate or that are not clearly communicated generally lead to misunderstandings, setting undesirable precedents or charges of favoritism. Thus, clear communications are essential. Also, if procedures or rules need to be changed, document the changes and update the procedures.

To Do: Know when exceptions should be made. When they are made, do it the right way with appropriate justification, good documentation and clear communications.

Notes:

eXPECTATIONS *Success Factor 94*

Working Definition: Yes, it's here twice! See Success Factor #22. Expectations are really that important so they're here again towards the end of our study together.

Success Factor: When defining the work to be done, identify those key expectations for every employee and clearly communicate them.

Application: Do it NOW!

Verse to Consider: Micah 6:8

Being More Successful: Your life will be simpler and smoother at work when expectations for each employee are clearly defined and communicated.

To Do: List your employees by name and the expectations for each, then tell them.

Notes:

eXpenses   Success Factor 95

Working Definition: Costs. Measured in money.

Success Factor: Effective managers know the costs associated with their products or services. Otherwise, how can you ever know your profit? Successful organizations pay close attention to expenditures.

Application: Identify and categorize all the costs in your business. At a minimum know the costs of producing a "good" product or service. (Don't forget the costs of maintenance!)

Verse to Consider: Luke 14: 28-30

Being More Successful: Have I clearly identified and quantified all the costs in my business?

To Do: Write out the steps you can take to identify and control costs. Implement them. An example could be as simple as recycling printer cartridges at a store that gives a ream of paper for the used cartridge; or as complex as forming a facility energy conservation team to implement action items to reduce energy consumption ($$).

Notes:

Davis Woodruff, PE, CMC

Yes   *Success Factor 96*

Working Definition: A general term of agreement, but more recently an expression of enthusiasm and excitement.

Success Factor: Too often a manager's first reply to new ideas is NO. Try "yes" instead—you'll be amazed at the results.

Application: Look for ways to get to "yes" instead of "no." Explore ideas with employees. Allow ideas to develop towards "yes." Be careful not to extinguish the spark of a new idea, encourage the spark to grow into a flame.

Verse to Consider: Acts 4:20

Being More Successful: Am I guilty of looking for ways to get to "no" instead of "yes?" Do I tend to "throw cold water" on new ideas an employee brings to me? In the interest of creativity, don't fall into the trap of being a "devil's advocate" or "naysayer" whenever a new idea arises.

To Do: Look for ways get to "yes."

Notes:

YESTERDAY *Success Factor 97*

Working Definition: Anytime previous to today.

Success Factor: We can only live today and plan for the future. Successful managers learn from yesterday and apply the Success Factors to today. You cannot manage history.

Application: Don't spend your time (Success Factor #83) trying to manage yesterday. Learn from yesterday, plan for the future and implement your plans.

Verse to Consider: Ecclesiastes 3:11

Being More Successful: How much time do I spend managing history? How can I be more effective in letting go of yesterday and getting busy for now and tomorrow? What did I learn from yesterday that I can use today?

To Do: Look for what you can do to more effectively plan and implement those plans for the future. Look at where you are trying to "manage history" and determine to eliminate these time wasters.

Notes:

YIELDING

Success Factor 98

Working Definition: Stepping back and not insisting on "your way or none" or not being bound by "the way we've always done it."

Success Factor: It is important to learn when it's necessary to yield your perceived rights to another person or department for the good of the entire organization. Getting rid of selfishness is another way to describe this success factor.

Application: Look for the time when you are insisting on your way or none; or when you are being bound by "the way we've always done it." Sometimes one cannot yield, for example when it comes to values and integrity. Sometimes you may just be selfish or stubborn if you won't yield to another person or department.

Verses to Consider: Philippians 2:3-4

Being More Successful: When decisions and actions are required, be guided by what is good for the entire organization, not just your interests or your department. Be willing to yield your own interests to those of the organization, unless it involves a conflict with your values or integrity.

To Do: Yield when you can, but know when not to yield.

Notes:

Youth   *Success Factor 99*

Working Definition: Anyone ten years or more younger than you are.

Success Factor: As the "boomers" begin to age out of the work force, the successful organizations recognize the need for developing the next generation of managers.

Application: Recognize the "rising stars" in your organization. Provide opportunities for them to make decisions and progress to the next level in the business. Help them understand what it takes to succeed as a manager in your organization. Teach them what they need to know about the organization. Impart as much of your "institutional knowledge" as possible.

Verse to Consider: I Timothy 4:12

Being More Successful: Identify the "youth" in your organization and the possible growth opportunities for them within the next 3—5 years. Provide them the chance to prepare for these positions that may be available to them in the coming years.

To Do: Make your list. Talk to those on the list. Prepare the next generation of managers while you have the chance to do it. Don't consider it a threat, but instead let it be your legacy.

Notes:

ZEAL
Success Factor 100

Working Definition: Fervor and enthusiasm for work.

Success Factor: When zeal is gone it's time to look for another job, before you destroy yourself or your business. At the least it's time to take off for a few days or weeks to get refocused on the work to be done.

Application: Effective managers approach work with enthusiasm, or passion, and passes it along to the employees.

Verse to Consider: Colossians 3:23

Being More Successful: Am I still enthusiastic about the work to be done? If not, what do I need to do now?

To Do: List several immediate action steps you can take in your behavior that will demonstrate your enthusiasm to your employees.

Notes:

Zip

Success Factor 101

Working Definition: Acting with speed, but in control. (Sometimes it's what we need to do with our mouth, as in "zip it shut.")

Success Factor: In today's economy speed is as important as cost and quality. Performance barriers must be identified and removed, especially those that relate to how customers do business with you.

Application: Identify performance barriers in your organization and take steps to eliminate them. Practice acting with ZIP—controlled speed.

Verse to Consider: Ecclesiastes 3:17

Being More Successful: Do I know the barriers that slow us down as an organization? How can we eliminate them?

To Do: Do something today to speed up the work in your area. Record what you did. Continue it tomorrow and the next day. Make it a habit to look for ways to improve. This is simply practicing continual improvement.

Notes:

Summary

Now that you've worked through these 101 Success Factors on management and leadership, what 5 things have you learned and applied that helped you most in your job? How have they helped you?

What will be your next steps to improve your practice of management and leadership?

Review the 101 Success Factors. What is the one thing that has helped you and your employees the most?

Have you completed your success plan for being a more effective manager? If not, why? If not, when?

As you've considered the various verses that were listed along with these management success factors, perhaps you have realized that you would like to know more about the God of the Bible. Let me quickly summarize several great truths for you to consider: God loves you, sent His Son to die on a cross that we might have eternal life, and wants to have a relationship with you. Here are several more verses to consider: John 3:16; Romans 3:23; Romans 6;23; Ephesians 2:8-9; Isaiah 53:6; John 1:1,14; Revelation 3:30; John 1:12 and John 6:47. Studying these verses and responding to them could make an eternal difference in your life now and forever.

END NOTES

[1] *How to Improve Human Performance*, Thomas K. Connellan, p.28, Harper and Row, 1978.

[2] Edwina Watkins, perhaps the world's best first grade teacher, West Decatur Elementary, 1984

[3] Tony Corley, retired Monsanto Plant Manager

[4] "Seven Steps to Better Employee Relations," *Supervisory Management*, Davis Woodruff, AMA

[5] Holy Bible, NIV, Zondervan, Proverbs 10:4

[6] Somers White, 1995, Scottsdale, AZ

MY SUCCESS PLAN
MY PLAN FOR BECOMING A MORE EFFECTIVE MANAGER

#	Factor	Date	Action Steps
1	Achievement		
2	Action		
3	Alternatives		
4	Attitude		
5	Balance		
6	Barriers		
7	Behavior		
8	Belief		
9	Budgets		
10	Change		
11	Commitment		
12	Communication		
13	Customer		
14	Data		
15	Decisiveness		
16	Delegation		
17	Details		
18	Discipline		
19	Employees		
20	Empowerment		
21	Evaluation		
22	Expectations		
23	Failures		

#	Factor	Date	Action Steps
24	Fairness		
25	Follow-up		
26	Future		
27	Go		
28	Goals		
29	Generosity		
30	Give		
31	Habits		
32	Harassment		
33	Honesty		
34	Humility		
35	Information		
36	Initiative		
37	Innovation		
38	Integrity		
39	Jargon		
40	Jealousy		
41	Jobs		
42	Justice		
43	Keep		
44	Kindness		
45	Leadership		
46	Learn		
47	Leave		
48	Listen		
49	Management		

#	Factor	Date	Action Steps
50	Measurement		
51	Money		
52	Motivation		
53	Neglect		
54	Never's		
55	New		
56	Notice		
57	Observe		
58	Once		
59	Organizing		
60	Overkill		
61	Performance		
62	Planning		
63	Preparation		
64	Procedures		
65	Processes		
66	Quality		
67	Quandaries		
68	Questions		
69	Regulations		
70	Reinforcement		
71	Relationships		
72	Resources		
73	Respect		
74	Resolve		
75	Results		

#	Factor	Date	Action Steps
76	Serve		
77	Sincerity		
78	Solutions		
79	Staffing		
80	Teach		
81	Technology		
82	Termination		
83	Time		
84	Uncertainty		
85	Understanding		
86	Values		
87	Variation		
88	Vision		
89	Waste		
90	Willingness		
91	Wisdom		
92	Work		
93	eXceptions		
94	eXpectations		
95	eXpenses		
96	Yes		
97	Yesterday		
98	Yielding		
99	Youth		
100	Zeal		
101	Zip		

About the Author

Davis M. Woodruff, an internationally recognized consultant, has authored over three dozen nationally published articles. His works have appeared in national and trade publications, as well as the prestigious Encyclopedia of Chemical Engineering. Taking Care of the Basics is a result of Davis researching success factors for managers during three decades in the real world.

Davis grew up on a family farm in rural southern Alabama where his family also owned a "country store." He was valedictorian of his class at Marion Military Institute and earned an engineering degree from Auburn University. He is a Professional Engineer and Certified Management Consultant. He was a manufacturing executive with 3M before forming his own consulting company, Management Methods, now in its third decade. Davis has shown over 120 organizations from Vermont to Malaysia how to be the low cost high quality producer in their industry.

Davis and Lynn were married in 1970. They have two daughters, one son-in-law and one grandson. He is active in his church and community; but is a husband, father and grandfather first and foremost.

You may contact Davis concerning his speaking and consulting by email or phone. Email: davisw@managementmethods.com or phone 256-355-3896. Snail mail goes to P.O. Box 1484, Decatur, AL 35602.

Printed in the United States
75030LV00005B/58-66